Houses

Written by David Drew
Illustrated by Dominique Falla

Some houses are made of brick.

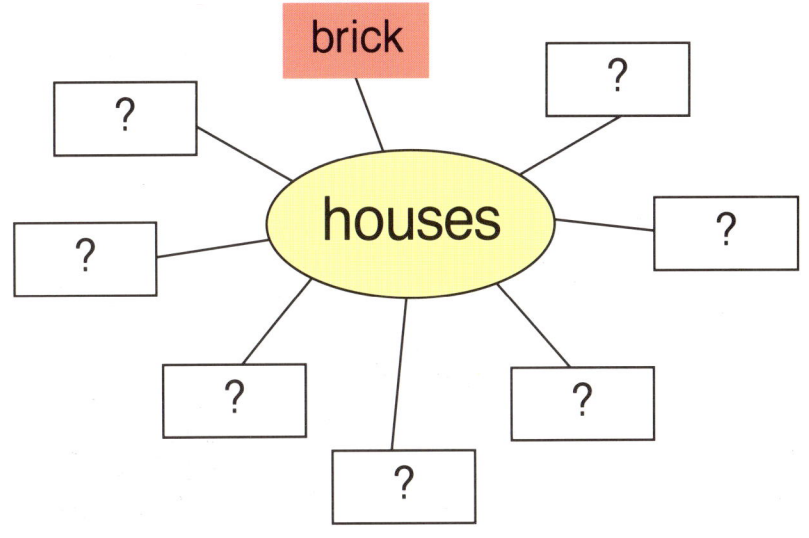

3

Some houses are made of stone.

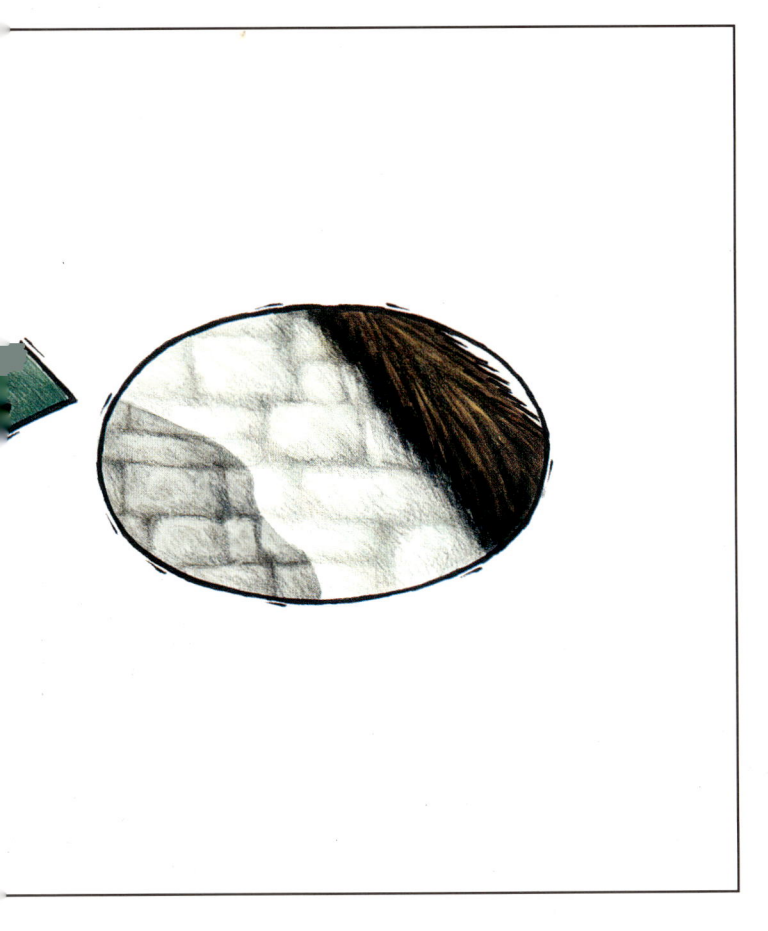
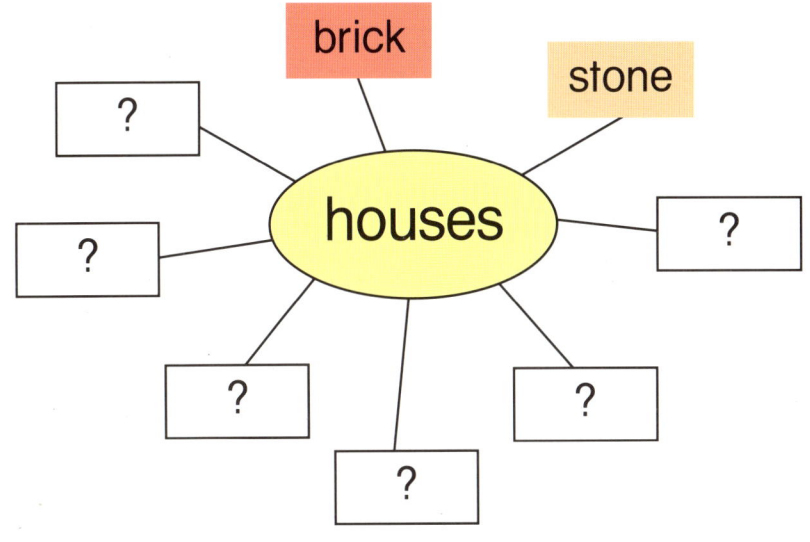

Some houses are made of metal.

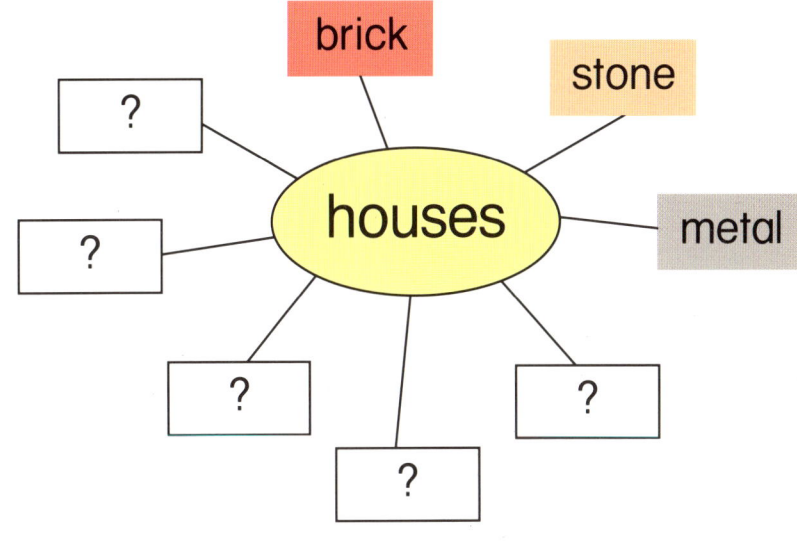

Some houses are made of clay.

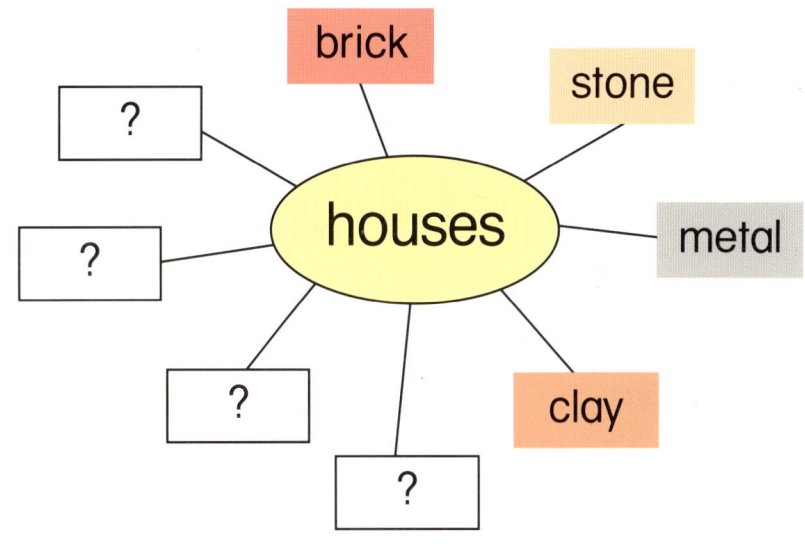

Some houses are made of ice.

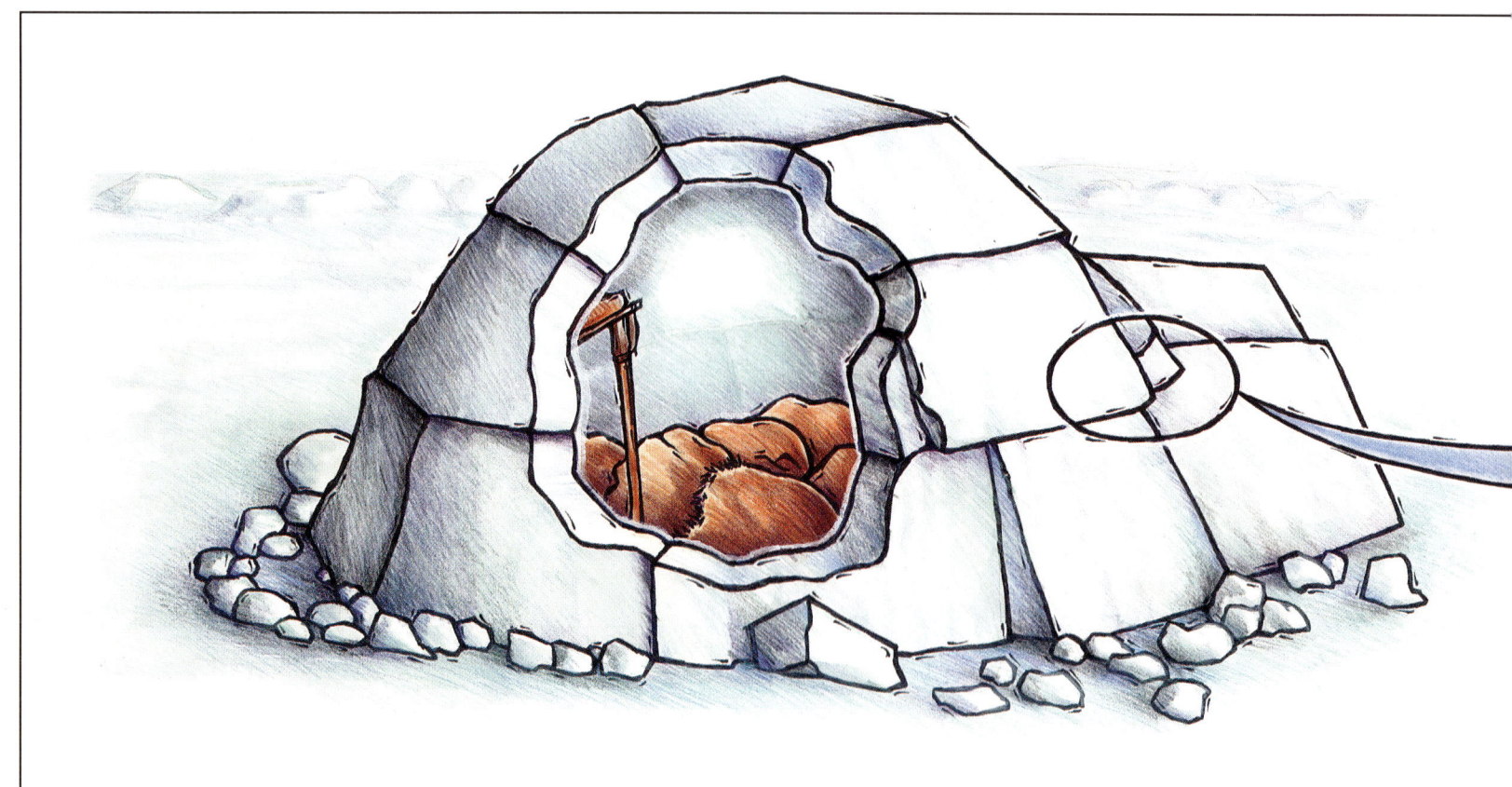

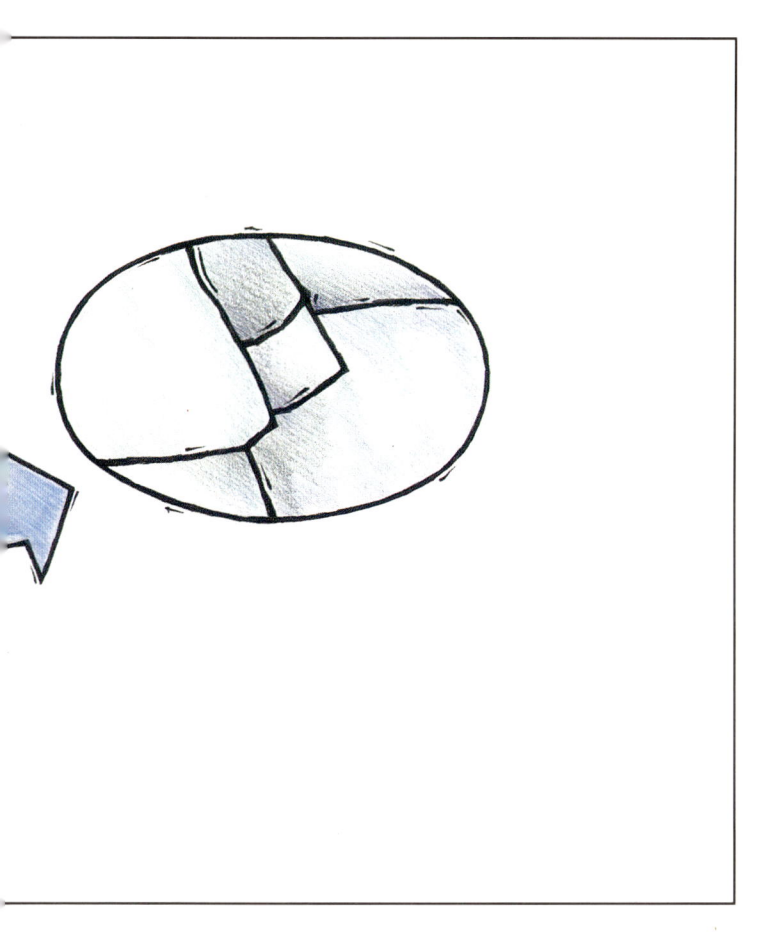
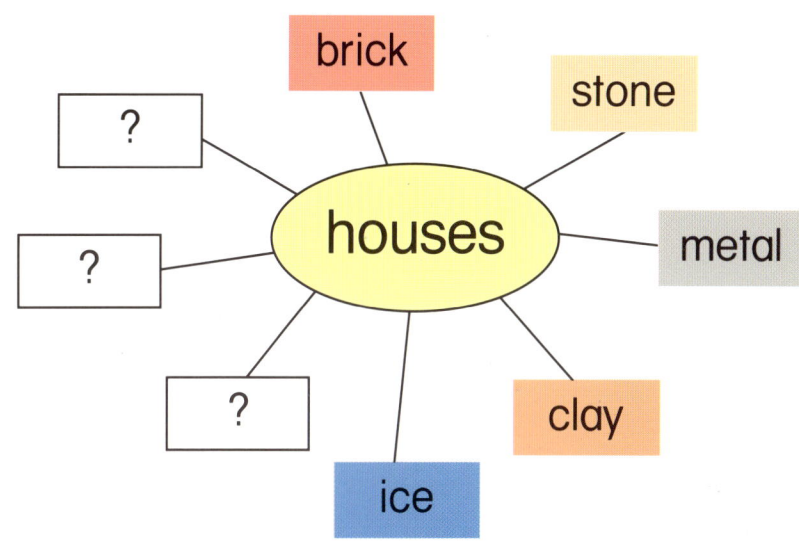

Some houses are made of wood.

12

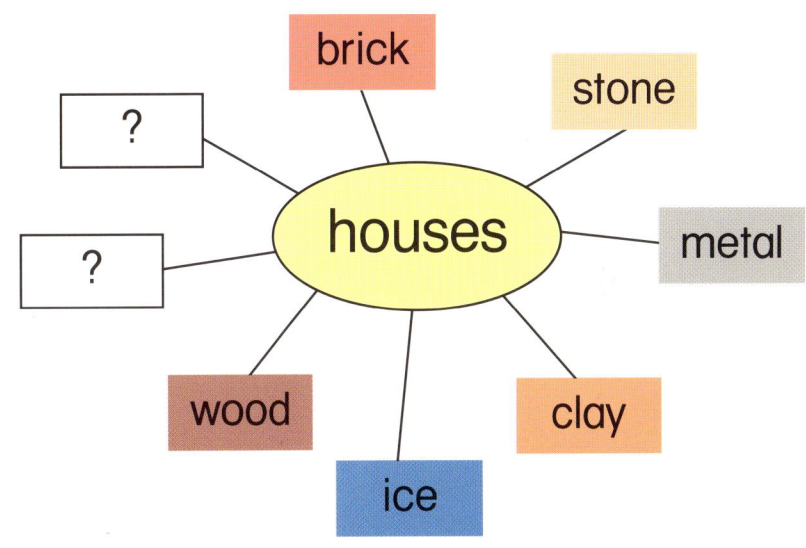

Some houses are made of cloth.

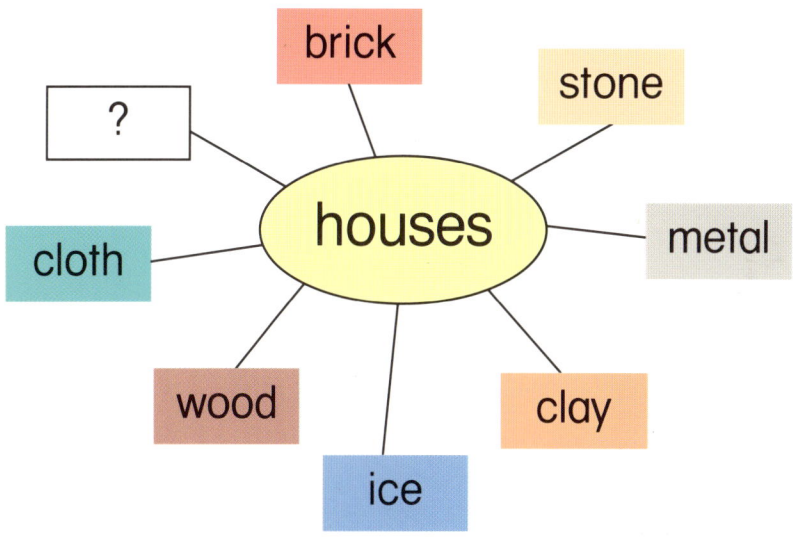

15

HOUSES AROUND THE WORLD

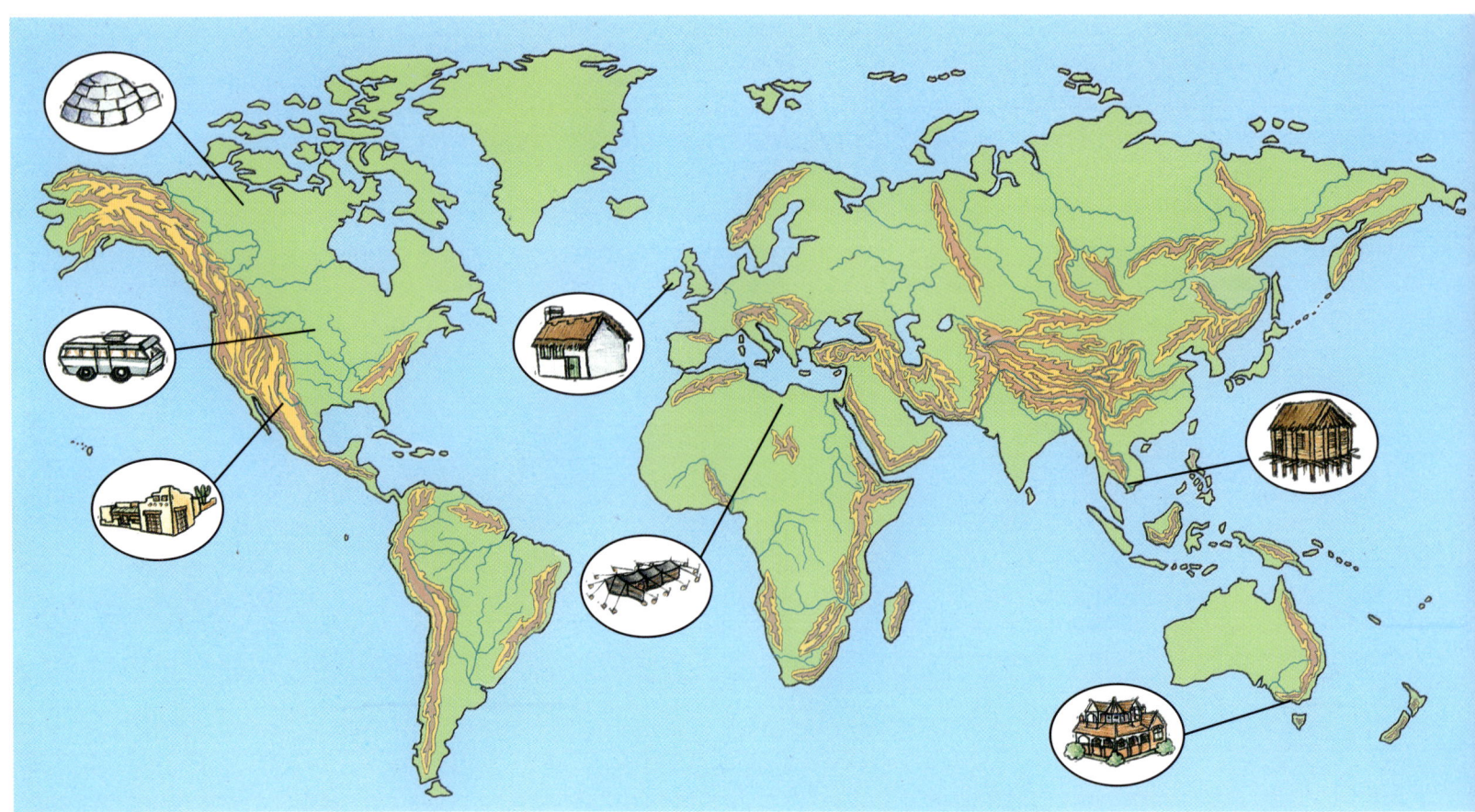

16